BRAZIL TRAVEL GUIDE 2023

Explore the Marvels of Brazil: A Comprehensive Travel Guide with Insider Tips, Discover Rio de Janeiro, Amazon Rainforest, Vibrant Culture, Hidden Gems and Must-See sights

James J. Johnson

All rights reserved. No part of this publication may be reproduced, distributed, or transmitted in any form or by any means, including photocopying, recording, or other electronic or mechanical methods, without the prior written permission of the publisher, except in the case of brief quotations embodied in critical reviews and certain other noncommercial uses permitted by copyright law.

Copyright © James J. Johnson, 2023

Table of Contents

My Vacation Story in Brazil
Introduction
    Climate and Geography
    Overview of culture
    Entry requirements and visas
    Exchange rates and money
    Communication through Language
Chapter 1: 10 Must-See Attractions
    Rio de Janeiro's Christ the Redeemer statue
    Falls in Iguazu and Paraná
    Manaus, Amazon Rainforest
    Salvador's Old Town -- Bahia
    Wetlands of the Pantanal in Mato Grosso, Brazil
    Mountain Sugarloaf in Rio de Janeiro
    Pernambuco's Fernando de Noronha
    Minas Gerais Ouro Preto
    National Park of Lençóis Maranhenses - Maranhão
    Mato Grosso do Sul's Bonito
Chapter 2: Brazil Undiscovered Gems
    Bahia Chapada Diamantina
    Rio de Janeiro's Ilha Grande
    Ceará - Jericoacoara
    Rio de Janeiro, Paraty
    Goiás' Chapada dos Veadeiros
    Santa Catarina's Praia do Rosa
Chapter 3: Food and Drink Delights
    Traditional Brazilian Dish: Feijoada

    Amazonian superfood Aça Bowl
    Seafood stew known as moqueca
    Brazilian chocolate truffle Brigadeiro
    National Drink: Caipirinha
    Traditional sugarcane spirit Cachaça tasting

Chapter 4: Brazil Dining Out and Prices
    Options for Fine Dining
    Wallet-friendly Restaurants
    Markets for Street Food
    Average Meal Price
    Tipping Protocol
    Options for vegetarians and vegans

Chapter 5: Brazil Transportation and Cost
    Internal Flights
    Bus Systems
    City Systems
    Renting a car
    Ridesharing and cabs
    Cost of transportation

Chapter 6: Accommodations and the cost
    Upscale inns and resorts
    Design-focused boutique hotels
    Affordable Accommodations
    Guesthouses and Hostels
    Holiday Rentals
    Average cost of lodging

Chapter 7: Itinerary for Two Weeks
    Rio de Janeiro on Days 1-3

- 4-6 days: Salvador
- Manaus and the Amazon Rainforest, days 7-9
- Iguazu Falls, Day 10–12
- 13-14th day: So Paulo

Chapter 8: Markets and Shopping
- Local crafts and artwork
- Gifts and Memorabilia
- Favored shopping areas
- Native American Crafts
- Outdoor markets
- Etiquette and Tips for Bargaining

Chapter 9: Health and safety Information
- Medical Precautions and Vaccinations
- Hospital emergency services
- Travel Protection
- Food and Water Safety
- Crime Prevention and Awareness
- Safety precautions and natural hazards

Chapter 10: Festivals and Cultural Experiences
- Carnival festivities
- Capoeira Performances
- Visits to Indigenous Communities
- Samba Music and Schools
- Folk dances and traditional music
- Religious Celebrations and Festivals

Chapter 11: Brazil Practical Details
- Local traditions and manners
- Portuguese phrases you should know

- Climate and Travel Advice
- Outlets and Adapters for Electricity
- Communication and the Internet
- Travel apps and resources

Conclusion
- Final advice and suggestions
- Accept Brazil's Dynamic Spirit
- Taking Stock of Your Journey
- Tell Us About Your Travels
- Recognition & Credits
- Boa Viagem e goodbye!

My Vacation Story in Brazil

My soul was forever changed by my exhilarating journey to Brazil, a country famed for its colorful culture, magnificent scenery, and various ecosystems. From the bustling streets of Rio de Janeiro to the verdant Amazon rainforest, this trip revealed the true spirit of Brazil through a kaleidoscope of remarkable experiences.

My voyage started in the busy metropolis of Rio de Janeiro, where the contagious energy that radiated from its vivid streets immediately captured my attention. It was awe-inspiring to see the recognizable Christ the Redeemer statue atop Corcovado Mountain, which provided sweeping views of the city's expansive beaches and lush landscapes. I couldn't resist the urge to visit the well-known Copacabana and Ipanema beaches, where the crystalline waters, golden sands, and rhythmic samba beats formed a blissful mood.

I entered Santa Teresa, a bohemian district in Rio, to learn more about the city's rich cultural diversity. Here, cobblestone alleys adorned with vibrant colonial architecture led me to charming art galleries, tiny cafés, and breathtaking views. I engaged myself in the throbbing nightlife while exploring the bustling neighborhoods of Lapa and Centro, dancing to the contagious sounds of samba, and savoring the delectable Brazilian cuisine.

I set off on an amazing trek into the heart of the Amazon jungle after leaving the metropolitan surroundings behind. I was completely in amazement as I delved deeper into this magnificent ecology. The incredibly diverse ecosystem of the Earth was demonstrated by the lush green canopy, which was bustling with life. I traveled over tangled pathways and came upon a variety of unusual animals, including colorful macaws, amusing monkeys, and elusive jaguars.

I had the opportunity to observe the daily cycles of nature while residing in a basic lodge amidst a tropical jungle. I took fantastic river excursions along the enormous Amazon River and its tributaries, waking up to the symphony of bird singing. A highlight was swimming with friendly pink river dolphins; their elegant presence humbled me in the presence of the area's natural splendor. During nighttime excursions, bioluminescent organisms shine an ethereal glow over the black waters, creating a captivating spectacle.

As I continued on my journey, I had Salvador da Bahia in mind. This city is rich in Afro-Brazilian heritage and has a thriving cultural legacy. I dug into the complex tapestry of African rhythms, colorful architecture, and mesmerizing street acts as I strolled through Pelourinho, a UNESCO World Heritage site. I was enticed to join in and take in the harmony of movement and song by the throbbing beats of capoeira, a martial art form blended with dance.

I devoured traditional meals like acarajé, a delicious deep-fried ball of black-eyed pea dough filled with shrimp and palm oil, as I immersed myself in the gastronomic wonders of Bahia. Ax music, a style that originated in Salvador, had rhythms that I couldn't resist as I joined locals in raucous street celebrations of life.

I found myself lured to the breathtaking majesty of Iguazu Falls, a natural wonder crossing the border between Brazil and Argentina, leaving the energetic streets of Salvador in my wake. I stood in awe at the majesty of nature as the thunderous roar of cascading water flooded the air with hazy rainbows. I marveled at the panoramic panoramas of this incredible show as I explored the several trails and platforms, documenting each moment with my camera.

My trip to Brazil was a symphony of hues, noises, and feelings that left a lasting impression on my heart. This journey immersed me in the beauty and diversity that constitute Brazil, from the energetic streets of Rio de Janeiro to the untamed wilderness of the Amazon jungle and the mesmerizing Afro-Brazilian culture in Salvador da Bahia. This amazing nation has deepened my appreciation for the beauties of nature and the diversity of human culture in addition to enhancing my awareness of the world. Brazil has a special place in my heart and soul, calling me back to discover even more of its stunning scenery and friendly people.

Introduction

Greetings from Brazil! Brazil, the largest country in South America, is a multicultural and dynamic country renowned for its beautiful natural scenery, extensive cultural history, and friendly people. Brazil provides a wide range of fascinating experiences that will captivate you, whether you choose to explore the pristine beaches along the coastline, journey deep into the Amazon rainforest, or spend time exploring the vibrant streets of Rio de Janeiro. This thorough guide will cover a variety of topics, including Brazil's geography and climate, a brief description of its culture, admission and visa formalities, money and exchange rates, and language and communication.

Climate and Geography

Brazil is distinguished by its extensive and diverse terrain, which includes the Pantanal wetlands, the beautiful Iguazu Falls, the long coastline, and the central plateau. With the exception of Chile and Ecuador, every country in South America shares boundaries with the country. Brazil, which has a surface area of almost 8.5 million square kilometers, has a wealth of natural beauties to discover.

Brazil's climate varies greatly depending on the region. The northern region of the country, which includes the Amazon rainforest, is dominated by equatorial and tropical climates, where year-round high temperatures and humidity are the norm. The climate becomes more temperate and has four distinct seasons as one moves south. Tropical weather with hot, muggy summers and mild winters prevails in coastal regions like Rio de Janeiro and Salvador. With moderate wintertime temperatures and sporadic frosts, the southern portion has a subtropical climate.

Overview of culture

A vibrant tapestry of customs, music, dance, and cuisine can be found in Brazil, which is a cultural melting pot that combines influences from indigenous, European, African, and Asian cultures. Brazilians are renowned for being hospitable and pleasant, which fosters a welcoming environment for visitors. Festivals like Carnival, a brilliant celebration of music, dance, and ornate costumes that takes place in places all around Brazil, showcase the nation's rich cultural legacy.

Some of the well-known musical styles that originated in Brazil and are extremely ingrained in the culture of the country are forró, bossa nova, and samba. Brazilian food is also a fascinating blend of flavors, with regional specialties like churrasco (Brazilian barbeque) and feijoada (a substantial black bean stew with pig), as well as deep-fried dough balls stuffed with shrimp, that tempt both locals and tourists.

Entry requirements and visas

It's crucial to familiarize yourself with the visa and admission procedures before traveling to Brazil. For the most recent information, it is advised to contact the Brazilian embassy or consulate in your home country. The specifics may change based on your nationality. Citizens of several nations, including the United States, Canada, Australia, Japan, and the majority of European nations, do not require a visa to visit Brazil for up to 90 days as of my knowledge's cutoff date in September 2021.

But you must have a passport that is current and has at least six months left on it after your anticipated departure date. When you arrive, you will need to fill out an immigration form and give it to the immigration officials along with your passport. During your visit to Brazil, it is wise to retain a copy of your passport and other vital travel documents in a secure location.

Exchange rates and money

Brazilian Reals (BRL) are the country's legal tender. Banks, authorized exchange offices, and airports all around the nation offer currency exchange services. To ensure a fair exchange rate, it is advised to change your money at these authorized outlets. Although most tourist destinations, hotels, and restaurants take major credit cards, it is still advisable to have some cash on hand for smaller transactions and in case you come across businesses that do not.

It is wise to check the exchange rates before your journey because the Brazilian Real's value varies with other currencies. You can get up-to-date information via mobile apps and online currency converters. It's also important to note that some ATMs and banks might charge a cost for foreign transactions, so it's a good idea to check with your bank about any applicable fees before going to Brazil.

Communication through Language

Portuguese is Brazil's official language, and the vast majority of people there speak it. English speakers are typically found at tourist hotspots, upmarket hotels, and restaurants even though it is not as common as Portuguese. However, learning a few fundamental Portuguese words will help you converse with locals in less visited locations and improve your overall trip experience. Brazilians are appreciative of foreigners who try to communicate in their language and will frequently go over and above to help you.

To overcome language obstacles, carrying a small Portuguese phrasebook or using smartphone translation apps can be really helpful. Your interactions will be considerably improved and you will be able to get around the country easily if you learn the standard greetings, food ordering, and asking for directions. It's also crucial to remember that Portuguese pronunciation can differ significantly from English pronunciation, so if you initially find it difficult, don't give up. Even if your pronunciation is not great, the locals will still be grateful for your efforts.

Travelers can enjoy a wide range of experiences in Brazil, a mesmerizing location. Brazil has much to offer everyone, from its spectacular natural beauty to its lively cultural heritage. You will be well-equipped to set out on a memorable adventure across this stunning South American country if you are aware of the country's topography and climate, cultural quirks, visa procedures, currency and exchange rates, as well as language and communication suggestions. Pack your luggage, acclimate to Brazil's dynamic atmosphere, and get ready to make lifelong moments that you won't soon forget.

Chapter 1: 10 Must-See Attractions

Brazil, the biggest nation in South America, is well known for its magnificent natural scenery, lively culture, and famous landmarks. Brazil has a wide variety of outstanding sites that draw tourists from all over the world, from the majestic Christ the Redeemer statue in Rio de Janeiro to the spellbinding Iguazu Falls in Paraná. With the goal of assisting you in making the most of your Brazilian vacation, we will examine each of these top 10 attractions in detail in this in-depth guide.

Rio de Janeiro's Christ the Redeemer statue

Christ the Redeemer, who is perched atop Corcovado Mountain, is a well-known representation of Brazil. With its arms extended, this enormous statue guards the thriving metropolis of Rio de Janeiro. Visitors are rewarded to a panoramic view of the beautiful coastline, verdant mountains, and lively cityscape below from its lofty point. It is advised to take the antique cog train to the summit, which adds an element of adventure, in order to reach the top in order to properly appreciate this marvel. Visit right at dusk to witness the city's transformation into a shimmering spectacle for a truly wonderful experience.

Falls in Iguazu and Paraná

The Iguazu Falls, a natural wonder that awes visitors with its magnificence, are tucked between Brazil, Argentina, and Paraguay. It is one of the most impressive waterfall systems on the planet, with over 275 distinct falls stretched over almost 2 miles. Take a boat tour to go up close to the thundering cascades or explore the well-maintained walking trails, which lead to stunning views at every turn, to learn more about the falls. Consider staying at one of the hotels located inside the national park for a really immersive experience that will allow you to see the falls in all their serene and ethereal splendor.

Manaus, Amazon Rainforest

As the "lungs of the Earth," the Amazon Rainforest is an unmatched natural paradise. Manaus, the entrance to the Brazilian Amazon, provides a memorable experience amidst the unusual species and lush vegetation. Take a boat excursion through the narrow rivers, watch colorful birds and monkeys from observation platforms high in the trees, or go on a guided stroll through the dense jungle. Consider traveling to a remote tribal community to experience indigenous cultures firsthand and gain insight into their customs, rites, and sustainable way of life.

Salvador's Old Town -- Bahia

Brazil's rich Afro-Brazilian heritage is on full display in Salvador, the dynamic Bahia capital. A UNESCO World Heritage site, the city's Pelourinho Historic Center is a treasure trove of colonial architecture, lively music, and fascinating history. Take a leisurely stroll through the cobblestone streets, explore historical churches that are exquisitely decorated with gold leaf, and savor the mouthwatering flavors of Bahian food. Participating in traditional dance and music performances will give you the chance to fully experience the vibrant local culture.

Wetlands of the Pantanal in Mato Grosso, Brazil

The Pantanal, the biggest tropical wetland in the world, is a haven for animal enthusiasts. This biodiverse landscape, which can be found in the state of Mato Grosso do Sul, is home to a staggering variety of plants and animals. Join a guided safari to see jaguars, caimans, capybaras, and a wide variety of bird species. The dry season (May to September) is the greatest time to travel because wildlife is concentrated around the remaining water sources due to the receding rivers. To really appreciate the splendor of this distinctive area, book a stay at one of the floating resorts or eco-lodges.

Mountain Sugarloaf in Rio de Janeiro

Sugarloaf Mountain (Po do Açcar), a striking natural formation rising steeply from Guanabara Bay's turquoise seas, is a well-known sight in Rio de Janeiro. Visitors take an exhilarating cable car ride to the summit, which provides amazing views of the city, the beaches, and the surrounding mountains. Sunset is an especially beautiful time to visit since the golden colors cast a mystical glow over the surroundings. Rock climbing or trekking to the top are options for the daring, both of which offer an exhilarating challenge and a sense of success.

Pernambuco's Fernando de Noronha

A hidden jewel of unmatched beauty, Fernando de Noronha is an archipelago off the northeastern coast of Brazil. This unspoiled paradise is a UNESCO World Heritage site and is renowned for its turquoise waters, white sand beaches, and abundant marine life. Visit vibrant coral reefs while snorkeling or scuba diving, interact with playful dolphins and sea turtles, or just relax on the isolated beaches. In order to secure a space in this tropical paradise, it is crucial to plan and make reservations well in advance because of the sensitive ecosystem there.

Minas Gerais Ouro Preto

Ouro Preto, located in the Minas Gerais hills, is a working museum of colonial buildings and baroque artwork. This lovely town, which served as a hub for the Brazilian gold rush, is known for its elaborate balconies, cobblestone walkways, and wonderfully preserved churches. Visit the old churches, like the So Francisco de Assis Church, which is well-known for its exquisite sculptures by Aleijadinho. Visit museums and galleries to fully appreciate the town's creative legacy, or simply relish the regional fare in one of the charming eateries lining the winding lanes.

National Park of Lençóis Maranhenses - Maranhão

The Lençóis Maranhenses National Park, which is located in northeastern Brazil, is a bizarre terrain of enormous sand dunes and pure freshwater lagoons. The dunes gather rainwater throughout the rainy season (from February to May), creating innumerable crystal-clear lagoons throughout the sandy expanse. Join guided treks or exhilarating 4x4 excursions to experience this distinct ecosystem's unearthly splendor. The park provides countless opportunities for photographers to take breath-taking pictures of the interaction between light, shadow, and the vivid blue hues of the lagoons.

Mato Grosso do Sul's Bonito

The town of Bonito, which translates to "beautiful" in Portuguese, is tucked away in the middle of the Brazilian Midwest and lives true to its name. This little village is well-known for its sparkling rivers, beautiful caves, and a wide variety of aquatic life. If you want to see the fascinating underwater world with its vibrant fish, submerged woods, and limestone structures, go snorkeling or scuba diving in the Rio da Prata or Sucuri River. Don't pass up the chance to tour the magnificent Blue Lake Cave or the Abismo Anhumas, which features a subterranean lake encircled by breathtaking stalactites and stalagmites.

Due to its enormous size and varied topography, Brazil has a wide range of attractions to suit the tastes of all tourists. Brazil never ceases to amaze, from the renowned Christ the Redeemer in Rio de Janeiro to the natural wonders of the Amazon Rainforest and the Pantanal Wetlands. These top 10 sites offer an exceptional look into the depth and complexity of Brazil's natural and cultural history, whether you're looking for adventure, cultural immersion, or simply leisure amidst stunning beauty. Join us on this adventure and let Brazil's wonders enchant your senses and leave you with lasting memories.

Chapter 2: Brazil Undiscovered Gems

Travelers looking for off-the-beaten-path locations will find a wealth of hidden gems in Brazil, a country famous for its dynamic cities, magnificent scenery, and rich culture. Every year, millions of tourists flock to well-known locations like Rio de Janeiro and the Amazon jungle, but there are other lesser-known locations that are equally alluring. This essay will examine six undiscovered Brazilian destinations that are beautiful in nature, serene, and provide interesting experiences. Let's take a journey across Brazil's undiscovered gems, from the ethereal vistas of Chapada Diamantina to the immaculate beaches of Praia do Rosa.

Bahia Chapada Diamantina

Chapada Diamantina, a mysterious wonderland with craggy mountains, clear rivers, and alluring waterfalls, is located in the center of the state of

Bahia. For those who enjoy the outdoors, this hidden gem provides a variety of activities, such as trekking, caving, and swimming in natural pools. The Chapada Diamantina National Park, a vast protected area with a total area of more than 1,500 square kilometers, serves as the focal point of the area. Visitors can discover breathtaking sights inside the park, like the Fumaça Waterfall, which cascades down a dizzying cliff and produces an ethereal mist that can be seen for kilometers.

The Gruta da Lapa Doce is a must-see for those with an adventurous spirit. This vast network of caves offers a surreal experience with its amazing rock formations and underground lakes. The Poco Azul, a magnificent underground lake with blue waters that are crystal transparent, is another highlight. You may explore the captivating underwater world in Poco Azul while snorkeling, which is studded with stalactites and submerged tree trunks.

In addition to the region's natural splendors, Chapada Diamantina is home to charming villages like Lençóis and Mucugê where tourists may immerse themselves in the area's rich history, sample local cuisine, and experience the friendly hospitality of the residents. Whether you're a thrill seeker or a nature enthusiast, Chapada Diamantina is sure to make an impression.

Recommendations:

Don't miss the sunrise at the spectacular overlook Morro do Pai Inácio, which gives expansive views of the surrounding mountains.
Bring along lightweight outdoor gear and comfortable hiking shoes.
To discover the area's secret trails and learn about its flora, animals, and geology, hire a competent guide.
Attending traditional music and dance performances in Lençóis is a great way to learn about the culture there.

Rio de Janeiro's Ilha Grande

Ilha Grande, an island off the coast of the state of Rio de Janeiro, is a tropical haven distinguished by lush jungles, immaculate beaches, and a relaxed environment. This island treasure is a car-free area, guaranteeing tourists a serene and eco-friendly setting to unwind and reconnect with nature. Every traveler may find something to do outside on Ilha Grande, which has more than 100 beaches and several hiking routes.

Lopes Mendes Beach, frequently praised as one of Brazil's most beautiful beaches, is one of the island's attractions. Its picture-perfect backdrop for relaxation and sunbathing is created by its pure white beach and blue waters. Adventurers can reach the Pico do Papagaio, a strenuous trip that rewards climbers with spectacular panoramic views of Ilha Grande, by hiking through the island's deep forests.

The island's diverse undersea environment will enthrall marine aficionados. Scuba diving and snorkeling reveal vivid coral reefs packed with fish of all hues, sea turtles, and, if you're lucky, dolphins. A well-liked location for snorkeling is the adjacent Blue Lagoon (Lagoa Azul), where you may discover marine life and swim in clean waters.

Vila do Abrao, the island's principal village, has a variety of lodging choices, from inviting guest houses to opulent eco-resorts. The community also has attractive eateries that serve up local specialties and fresh seafood, giving visitors a true experience of Brazil's coastal region.

Recommendations:

Explore the island by boat to find undiscovered coves, beaches, and snorkeling locations.
Observe the island's environmental regulations and support its sustainability initiatives.
Visit the Aqueduto Ruins, an old monument from the island's colonial past.

Experience the island's eco-lodges for a one-of-a-kind and all-encompassing encounter with nature.

Ceará - Jericoacoara

The modest fishing community of Jericoacoara, sometimes known as Jeri, is tucked away on Brazil's northeastern coast and has been transformed into a popular beach resort. The magnificent sand dunes, clean lagoons, and powerful winds that characterize this secluded paradise make it a refuge for lovers of water sports, especially windsurfers and kitesurfers.

The Sunset Dune is one of Jericoacoara's most recognizable sights, drawing tourists there each evening to take in the breathtaking Atlantic Ocean sunset. The sky is painted with vivid shades of orange and pink as the sun sets, creating a magnificent ambience that is best experienced while sipping a delicious caipirinha.

The most well-known of Jericoacoara's natural lagoons is the Lagoa Azul (Blue Lagoon).

Swimmers can enjoy the unique and amazing sensation of swimming in transparent blue seas while being surrounded by sand dunes that reach the sky. Similar surroundings can be found at the nearby Lagoa do Paraiso (Paradise Lagoon), with its picture-perfect palm trees and hammocks dangling over the lake, making it the ideal place to unwind.

Jericoacoara, in addition to its natural attractions, has a vibrant nightlife with a variety of beach bars, live music venues, and street parties. The village's sandy streets, where visitors can browse boutiques, art galleries, and local craft shops, add to its rustic beauty.

Recommendations:

Attempt windsurfing or kiteboarding by receiving lessons from a knowledgeable local instructor.
A buggy tour of the neighborhood will allow you to discover secret lagoons, distant beaches, and striking rock formations.

Try some of the regional cuisine, especially the seafood specialties and other classic northeastern meals.

Start a horseback riding adventure to explore the dunes and see the breathtaking scenery from a fresh angle.

Rio de Janeiro, Paraty

Paraty is a colonial gem with a rich history and beautiful natural surroundings, nestled between luscious mountains and the sparkling waters of the Costa Verde. The state of Rio de Janeiro's lovely town is well known for its restored Portuguese colonial architecture, cobblestone alleys, and thriving cultural scene.

The ancient district of Paraty, a UNESCO World Heritage site, is a labyrinth of winding alleyways dotted with vibrant colonial structures, art galleries, and inviting cafés. As the primary form of transportation, horse-drawn carriages add to the town's beautiful and nostalgic atmosphere, exploring this area feels like going back in time.

Paraty is surrounded by a network of islands, isolated beaches, and lush rainforests, which, in addition to their architectural splendor, provide countless options for outdoor excursions. Visitors can snorkel in crystal-clear waters, unwind on undeveloped beaches, and explore secret coves that can only be reached by boat when on boat tours to adjacent islands. Additionally, the area is littered with hiking routes that allow you to fully experience the Atlantic Forest, where you can find waterfalls, natural pools, and an incredible diversity of flora and animals.

The internationally acclaimed Paraty International Literary Festival (FLIP) is just one of the many cultural events that Paraty offers each year in addition to its natural beauty. The festival draws well-known writers, thinkers, and book enthusiasts from all over the world, transforming the town into a center for literary talks, poetry readings, and cultural events.

Recommendations:

Learn about the Party's history, architecture, and cultural legacy by taking a guided walking tour.

Tasting traditional fare like moqueca (a fish stew), feijoada (a black bean stew), and cachaça (a Brazilian sugarcane drink) can help you learn more about the regional cuisine.

Take your time discovering the quiet seas and undiscovered beaches by renting a kayak or paddleboard.

Take a day trip to the adjacent Serra da Bocaina National Park to go trekking, observe birds, and explore waterfalls.

Goiás' Chapada dos Veadeiros

Chapada dos Veadeiros, a sizable natural park in the center of Brazil, is well-known for its breathtaking scenery, calming atmosphere, and distinctive fauna. This undiscovered treasure is a haven for nature lovers and enlightenment seekers alike, offering a mesmerizing combination of waterfalls, gorges, quartz crystal formations, and broad savannas.

The Veadeiros Plateau, a sizable raised area covered with cerrado vegetation, is the focal point of Chapada dos Veadeiros. Here, travelers may set out on thrilling walks while taking in panoramic views of the neighboring valleys and coming across beautiful waterfalls. A must-see sight in the area is the Cachoeira Santa Bárbara, with its azure waters tumbling over moss-covered rocks.

The Vale da Lua (Moon Valley), a surreal environment formed by the erosion of quartzite rocks, is another feature of Chapada dos Veadeiros. With its unusual rock formations, constricting canyons, and natural ponds, walking through this lunar-like environment is like entering a foreign world. The area's mysterious atmosphere adds to its attractiveness and draws people looking for a closer connection to nature and themselves.

The village of Alto Paraíso de Goiás is the entryway to Chapada dos Veadeiros and has a variety of lodging options, including eco-retreats and rustic lodges. The town also acts as a center for spiritual and complementary therapies, with a number of establishments providing yoga lessons, meditation retreats, and complementary medical procedures.

Recommendations:

Explore the quaint neighborhood of So Jorge Village, home to artisan shops, regional handicrafts, and vegetarian eateries. It is close to Chapada dos Veadeiros.
Swim in the " Termais," or natural hot springs, which are thought to have therapeutic qualities.
Experience a stargazing tour at night to be amazed by the bright heavens of Chapada dos Veadeiros, a popular location for astronomy enthusiasts.
To protect the park's delicate ecosystems and reduce your environmental impact, abide by its laws and regulations.

Santa Catarina's Praia do Rosa

Praia do Rosa, a hidden gem located on Brazil's southern coast, is famed for its unspoiled beauty, immaculate beaches, and great surf. A haven for those seeking relaxation, nature, and water sports, this picturesque fishing community in the state of Santa Catarina offers a laid-back and bohemian ambiance.

The beach in Praia do Rosa, a crescent-shaped bay covered in golden sand and surrounded by lush green hills, is without a doubt the town's main draw. The beach is not simply a haven for sunbathers; it is also a well-known surfing location that draws surfers from all over the world. Whether you're a novice or an expert surfer, Praia do Rosa's reliable waves and perfect conditions will more than meet your surfing needs.

In addition to having waves that are good for surfing, Praia do Rosa is renowned for having a diverse ecosystem. Southern right whales, which are in risk of extinction, can be found in the

Atlantic Forest and nearby hills. Visitors have the opportunity to see these gorgeous animals up close from July to November when they move to the region for breeding and mating. A special opportunity to see whales up close and discover how to save them is provided through boat cruises.

The hamlet itself, with its boutique stores, organic cafés, and beachside bars, emanates a bohemian and laid-back attitude. Visitors can savor delectable seafood delicacies, sip caipirinhas while taking in the sunset, or just wander through the charming village's streets.

Recommendations:

Discover the neighboring Ibiraquera Lagoon, where you can go kayaking or stand-up paddling in the tranquil waters.
Hike along the coastal trails for breathtaking views of the cliffs, beaches, and ocean nearby.
At one of the eateries by the beach, indulge in a churrasco, a typical Brazilian barbeque.

Attend one of Praia do Rosa's numerous music festivals or cultural events to experience the area's thriving music scene and creative community.

Conclusion:

A wide variety of natural beauty, adventure, and cultural experiences can be had in Brazil's undiscovered gems. Each place has its own distinct fascination, from the ethereal landscapes of Chapada Diamantina and the remote beaches of Ilha Grande to the windswept dunes of Jericoacoara and the historical elegance of Paraty. Praia do Rosa offers a laid-back surf culture and unspoiled beauty, while Chapada dos Veadeiros enchants with its magnificent vistas and spiritual vitality. These undiscovered Brazilian treasures will leave you with priceless memories and a greater understanding of the nation's natural delights, whether you're looking for peace and quiet, excitement, or a mix of both. Pack your bags and set out on a remarkable journey to find these undiscovered gems that reveal Brazil in all its authentic glory.

Chapter 3: Food and Drink Delights

Brazilian food is a fascinating fusion of native, European, African, and Asian influences, creating an array of dishes that are rich and lively. Brazil offers a wide variety of delectable dishes and drinks that are adored by residents and sought after by tourists, ranging from hearty stews to tropical superfoods and reviving beverages. This thorough tour will go into some of the most well-known foods and drinks from Brazil, such as Feijoada, Aça Bowl, Moqueca, Brigadeiro, Caipirinha, and Cachaça sampling. Prepare to go off on a culinary adventure through Brazil's many cuisines.

Traditional Brazilian Dish: Feijoada

The pinnacle of Brazilian comfort cuisine is feijoada. It is a filling stew made with black beans that has its roots in African cooking. Feijoada is a dish that is typically prepared with black beans, various types of beef, and pig. A rich and hearty stew is produced by simmering the meats until they are soft and the flavors have had time to blend. Traditional accompaniments to feijoada include white rice, farofa (toasted manioc flour), collard greens, and orange slices, which offer a cooling counterpoint to the dish's richness. Feijoada tastes best when paired with a robust red wine or a refreshing caipirinha.

Recomendação: Visita "boteco" or "casa de feijoada," a typical Brazilian eatery, for a real feijoada experience. TrêsBar do Mineiro em Santa Teresa, Rio de Janeiro, e "Feijoada da Lana" na Vila Madalena district, São Paulo.

Amazonian superfood Aça Bowl

Aça, a fruit native to the Amazon rainforest that is high in antioxidants and other nutrients, has become well known throughout the world. In Brazil and other countries, aça bowls have gained popularity as a breakfast or snack alternative. Frozen aça berries are combined with a little liquid (such as coconut water) to provide a thick, creamy base for an aça bowl.

Granola, bananas, shredded coconut, and honey are added as toppings to boost flavor and offer a satisfying crunch. In addition to being tasty, aça bowls offer a revitalizing and invigorating start to the day.

Visit "Polis Sucos" in Ipanema, Rio de Janeiro, for their renowned aça bowls. Try "Tacacá do Norte" in Belém for an authentic and tasty aça experience if you're in the Amazon region.

Seafood stew known as moqueca

A bright and flavorful fish stew from Brazil's coast is called moqueca. Fresh fish, shrimp, or other seafood is cooked with onions, tomatoes, bell peppers, garlic, cilantro, coconut milk, and palm oil in this delectable dish. The stew turns out to be rich and fragrant as a result of the dish's slow cooking, which allows the flavors to mingle together. Traditional accompaniments to moqueca include white rice, farofa, and a side of piro (a rich fish gravy). This meal exemplifies how indigenous and African culinary traditions have influenced Brazilian cuisine.

Recommendation: For a fantastic moqueca experience while visiting Bahia, go to "Restaurante Donana" in Salvador. Visitei a Moquecaria do Joo" at Vitória in Espírito Santo to sample their famed moqueca capixaba.

Brazilian chocolate truffle Brigadeiro

The topic must be brought up in any discussion of Brazilian food. Brazilian festivals, parties, and dessert menus are not complete without these delectable chocolate truffles. Condensed milk, butter, cocoa powder, and chocolate sprinkles are the ingredients used to make . Sprinkles are added after the mixture is formed into bite-sized balls and fried until thick. A thick, fudgy, and deliciously chocolatey dessert that melts in your tongue is the end product. Any chocolate lover must try .

For a wide variety of tastes and exquisitely designed brigadeiros, seek out specialty brigadeiro stores like "Maria Brigadeiro" in Sao

Paulo or "Fabiana D'Angelo Brigadeiros" in Rio de Janeiro.

National Drink: Caipirinha

The iconic Brazilian drink, the caipirinha, is renowned for its tart and refreshing flavors. Cachaça (a Brazilian alcohol manufactured from sugarcane), fresh limes, sugar, and ice are used to make this famous beverage. Cachaça and ice are blended after the limes are mushed with sugar to release their juices and vital oils. As a result, the cocktail has the proper amount of sweetness and citrus flavor. Brazil is a country where caipirinhas are popular, from coastal shacks to hip bars in the busy cities.

Visit "Bar Veloso" for their renowned caipirinhas and lively environment in So Paulo. For a wide variety of cachaças to pick from, visit "Academia da Cachaça" in Leblon, Rio de Janeiro.

Traditional sugarcane spirit Cachaça tasting

Brazil's national spirit, cachaça, is made from fermented sugarcane juice. It has a significant role in Brazilian culture and is a vital component in caipirinhas. There are several varieties of cachaça, from unaged (branca) to barrel-aged (). You can discover the subtle differences between various cachaças while tasting them, learning about their production processes, maturing procedures, and flavor characteristics. Cachaça offers a diverse range of flavors to discover and enjoy, ranging from silky and floral to strong and smokey.

Visit the "Alambique Cachaçaria" in So Paulo for a thorough cachaça tasting experience. Knowledgeable staff members can lead you through the nuances of this well-known Brazilian liqueur.

Brazilian food is a kaleidoscope of vivacious tastes, cultural influences, and illustrious culinary traditions. The flavors of Brazil are as varied as the nation itself, ranging from the decadent feijoada to the hydrating aça bowl. To explore the depths of Brazilian culinary heritage, try meals like moqueca and . A fuller appreciation of the cultural significance of these libations can be gained by sipping a caipirinha or partaking in a cachaça tasting while enjoying these dishes. So make sure to taste the delicious foods and beverages that Brazil has to offer, whether you're in the crowded streets of Rio de Janeiro or the serene nooks of the Amazon rainforest.

Chapter 4: Brazil Dining Out and Prices

Brazil provides locals and visitors with a fantastic dining experience thanks to its vibrant culture and varied culinary traditions. Brazil offers plenty to please every palate, from upscale restaurants to inexpensive cafes and vibrant street food markets. We will examine the numerous dining options, typical meal prices, tipping customs, and the availability of vegetarian and vegan options across the nation in this complete guide.

Options for Fine Dining

Brazil has a vibrant fine dining scene that highlights the nation's superior cuisine. These restaurants offer a classy setting, flawless service, and a large selection of gourmet foods made with great care. Expect to pay between 150 and 500 Brazilian Reais (BRL) per person for a multi-course lunch, while the price of fine dining can vary based on the venue and location.

DOM (São Paulo): Under the direction of renowned chef Alex Atala, DOM is known throughout the world for its creative and affluent Brazilian cuisine. For foodies, the tasting menu, which features delicacies from the area, is a must-try.

Chef Claude Troisgros is the owner of Olympe in Rio de Janeiro, a restaurant renowned for fusing French and Brazilian cuisine. The eatery offers a classy dining experience with meals that masterfully combine regional ingredients with traditional French cooking methods.

Man (São Paulo): Man offers a remarkable eating experience by fusing modern methods with classic Brazilian flavors. Their food honors Brazil's culinary tradition and focuses on seasonal ingredients.

Wallet-friendly Restaurants

Brazil provides a variety of options, from intimate cafés to lovely neighborhood eateries, for tourists on a budget or those looking for a more relaxed eating experience. These restaurants offer delectable meals at reasonable prices without sacrificing flavor or quality. A dinner at a cheap restaurant typically costs between 15 and 40 BRL per person.

Brazilian classics like feijoada (black bean stew) and pastel (fried pastry) are served at the well-liked tavern and restaurant Boteco Belmonte in Rio de Janeiro. It is a preferred destination for both locals and visitors because of the laid-back environment and reasonable costs.

A Casa do Porco (São Paulo) is renowned for its pork-focused menu and serves a variety of mouthwatering foods, such as sandwiches, sausages, and pork belly. Despite its rising demand, the costs are still rather reasonable, giving it a great option for foodies on a tight budget.

Tapiocaria da Dinha in Salvador is the best place to enjoy this delicacy. Tapioca is a classic Brazilian meal prepared from cassava flour. This restaurant offers a tasty and affordable meal choice with a range of fillings like cheese, coconut, and savory meats.

Markets for Street Food

Feiras, or street food markets, are an essential component of Brazilian cuisine. These vivacious markets, where you can get anything from traditional snacks to regional specialties, provide a wide variety of flavors. Street food markets are a great option for getting a taste of the regional cuisine and discovering Brazil's true flavors. The typical price range for each item in these markets is 5 to 20 BRL.

Rio de Janeiro's Feira de So Cristovo is a vibrant market that honors the diverse cultural history of Northeastern Brazil. Live music and dance performances go together with local delicacies like acarajé (deep-fried black-eyed pea dough filled with shrimp) and carne de sol (sun-dried beef).

The ancient Mercado Municipal de São Paulo (So Paulo) is a haven for foodies. Visit several kiosks to sample pastries, exotic fruits, or the renowned mortadella sandwich. The codfish pastel, a favored local delicacy, should not be missed.

Mercado Modelo (Salvador): Mercado Modelo, a bustling market with a wide selection of street cuisine, is situated in the center of Salvador. Try the delectable acarajé, a deep-fried dough ball loaded with shrimp and spices, or sample some of the delicious moqueca (fish stew) and abará (steamed black-eyed pea cakes) that are characteristic Bahian dishes.

Average Meal Price

Planning your spending accordingly might be made easier if you are aware of the typical price of a meal in Brazil. Prices can change depending on the area, the type of restaurant, and the dishes purchased. The price ranges for typical meals at various restaurants are broken down as follows:

Fine Dining: A multi-course meal at a high-end restaurant will cost you anywhere between 150 and 500 BRL per person.

Mid-range Restaurants: The cost of a dinner at a moderately priced restaurant, which includes a main course and a non-alcoholic beverage, can range from 40 to 100 BRL per person.

Budget-friendly Restaurants: Cozy cafés and local eateries provide inexpensive options, with meals costing between 15 and 40 BRL per person.

Street cuisine: The cost of a single item for street cuisine often ranges between 5 and 20 BRL.

Tipping Protocol

Brazil's tipping customs may be different from those in other nations. Although not required, tips are welcomed for excellent service. Here are some tips to remember when tipping:

Restaurants: It is traditional to leave a tip at restaurants, especially if the service was good, of about 10% of the total cost. Check the bill before leaving a tip as certain restaurants could include a service charge (typically approximately 10%).

Bars: In Brazil, tipping bartenders is uncommon. However, rounding up the amount or leaving a little tip is welcomed if you experience great service or want to express your gratitude.

Taxis: While rounding up the fare is a normal practice, tipping taxi drivers is not required.

Other Services: Depending on the degree of service received, it is typical to tip bellhops, housekeeping workers, and concierge services at hotels.

Options for vegetarians and vegans

The food scene in Brazil offers vegetarian and vegan options to suit a variety of dietary requirements. Although meat is a major component of traditional Brazilian cuisine, many restaurants also offer vegetarian and vegan options. Additionally, there are more devoted vegetarian and vegan eateries in bigger cities like So Paulo, Rio de Janeiro, and Salvador.

Banana Verde (São Paulo): This renowned vegetarian eatery features a broad menu with inventive dishes that highlight Brazil's voluminous culinary traditions. Banana Verde offers a lovely dining experience with dishes like vegan feijoada and delectable desserts.

Teva (Rio de Janeiro): Teva is a vegan restaurant that combines local and foreign foods. Teva's menu features a variety of cutting-edge meals that are suitable for both vegetarians and vegans, with a focus on sustainability and ethical sourcing.

The historic center of Salvador is home to Orgânicos da Vila, a restaurant that serves organic vegetarian and vegan fare. Fresh, regionally-sourced foods are used on the menu, and the delectable plant-based options honor the region's culinary history.

The food scene in Brazil is a treasure trove of tastes, providing a wide variety of eating alternatives to suit every taste and budget. Brazil's diverse culinary scene will satisfy your cravings, whether you're looking for a high-end fine dining experience, a quick and inexpensive dinner, or the excitement of street food markets. The nation is embracing nutritional diversity and making sure that everyone can enjoy its culinary delights by placing an increased emphasis on vegetarian and vegan options. So get ready to explore Brazil's gastronomic delights and enjoy the distinctive flavors that this alluring nation has to offer.

Chapter 5: Brazil Transportation and Cost

Brazil is a sizable nation with a variety of landscapes, a rich cultural history, and bustling cities. Brazil provides a wide range of options for getting around, including domestic flights, bus networks, metro systems, auto rentals, taxis, and ridesharing services. We will examine each method of transportation in detail, go through their costs, and offer traveler recommendations in our extensive guide.

Internal Flights

Due to the size of Brazil, domestic flights are a common option for long-distance travel within the nation. Gol Linhas Aéreas, LATAM Airlines Brazil, and Azul Brazilian Airlines are just a few of the well-known carriers that fly within Brazil. Both large cities and more remote rural destinations are well-served by these airlines.

Costs: The price of domestic flights in Brazil varies depending on the route used, the timing of the reservation, and the airline of choice. In general, making reservations early and being flexible with your travel dates might help you get better rates. Long-haul flights, like those from Sao Paulo to Manaus, can cost between $200 and $500, while short-haul flights, like those from So Paulo to Rio de Janeiro, can cost anywhere between $50 and $150.

Recommendations:

In order to get the cheapest prices, plan and reserve your flights well in advance.
To locate the cheapest options, compare costs on several airlines and travel companies.
To possibly save money, think about flying on weekdays or outside of the busiest travel times.
Examine any additional charges, like luggage fees, as they can have a big impact on the final bill.

Bus Systems

Brazil has a robust and interconnected bus system, giving it an accessible and practical means of travel for both short and large distances. Brazil's bus system is dependable, comfortable, and popular with both locals and visitors.

Costs: Compared to domestic flights, bus travel in Brazil is typically less expensive. The distance traveled, the bus company, and the degree of comfort supplied all affect the fare. For instance, a quick trip inside a city may cost between $1 and $3, but intercontinental travel may cost between $10 and $50. The cost of luxury buses with greater facilities will increase.

Recommendations:

To locate dependable and comfortable solutions, read evaluations of various bus operators.
Particularly during periods of high travel demand, think about purchasing your bus tickets in advance.

For lengthy trips, use luxury or semi-luxury buses to ensure a more comfortable ride.

Buses have numerous stops along the journey, so plan for lengthier travel times, particularly for interstate excursions.

City Systems

Brazil's major cities, including So Paulo, Rio de Janeiro, and Brasilia, all have developed and effective metro systems. These elevated or underground rail systems offer a practical way to get around cities without being stuck in traffic.

Costs: Metro rides in Brazil are not too expensive. The prices are often depending on distance, with higher prices for longer trips. For instance, a single metro ride in So Paulo can cost between $1.20 and $3, whilst a daily pass might cost between $5 and $7.

Recommendations:

For convenience and potential cost savings, get a rechargeable metrocard, such as a Bilhete nico in Sao Paulo or a RioCard in Rio de Janeiro.

If at all possible, avoid peak hours because rush hour can be congested on the metro.

To make the most of your trip throughout the city, familiarize yourself with the metro map and plan your routes beforehand.

Renting a car

For those who want more freedom and independence or who want to explore rural areas, renting a car in Brazil can be a practical option. However, it's crucial to take into account elements like the volume of traffic, the state of the roads, and the price of fuel.

Costs: The price of renting a car in Brazil varies based on the type of vehicle, how long the rental is, and the location. Compact cars typically cost between $30 and $70 per day to hire, whereas larger cars or luxury cars might cost between $70 and $150 per day. The total cost should account for additional costs like fuel and insurance.

Recommendations:

To get the best bargain, compare prices offered by several automobile rental companies.
Examine the rental agreement's terms and conditions, particularly the insurance and mileage restrictions.
Learn the local rules and regulations governing traffic, and drive carefully, especially in crowded city centers.
To explore uncharted territory, think about renting a GPS or downloading a navigation app.

Ridesharing and cabs

Brazil has a large taxi and ridesharing industry, especially in urban regions. When you want a door-to-door service or for short trips, taxis are a practical solution. Like Uber and 99, ridesharing services are likewise well-liked and have affordable costs.

Costs: In Brazil, taxis usually have a basic fare and then a metered cost that changes with the distance and time. As a general rule, prices can range from $1.50 to $3 with an additional $0.75 to $1 every kilometer. Prices may vary significantly between cities. Depending on the provider and location, ridesharing services typically have comparable pricing structures.

Recommendations:

Utilize trustworthy taxi companies or authorized taxis from authorized taxi stands.
Compare costs for ridesharing services and select the most reputable and highly rated provider.
Before beginning the trip, confirm the fare with the driver, especially in taxis where there may not be a working meter.
Because drivers might not always have enough change for larger denominations, carry small banknotes or change.

Cost of transportation

Budgeting for travel costs is crucial while organizing a trip to Brazil. Here are some other things to think about:

baggage charges Check the baggage allowances and any potential airline surcharges before booking an aviation trip because carrying more than the allotted amount may result in additional fees.

Parking charges: If you decide to rent a car, be aware that these charges may be necessary in some towns or at certain tourist destinations. Include these extra costs in your budget plan.

Brazil has a vast network of toll roads, especially on the highways that connect its major cities. If you intend to drive between several locations, arrange for toll costs.

Consider the cost of fuel while hiring a car or using a ride-sharing service. Brazil's fuel costs might vary, but they are often less expensive than those in many other nations.

Brazil's transportation system offers a variety of options to accommodate various travel tastes and price ranges. Buses offer reliable and economical intercity transport whereas domestic flights are best for lengthy distances. Within big cities, metro systems are effective, and renting a car gives you freedom when exploring rural areas. For shorter trips, taxis and ridesharing services are practical. You may make the most of your transportation options in Brazil and improve your overall travel experience by taking into account the pricing, suggestions, and advance planning.

Chapter 6: Accommodations and the cost

Brazil, a vibrant and diverse nation in South America, provides a variety of lodging choices to fit any traveler's needs and price range. Brazil offers a wide variety of lodging options, from opulent hotels and resorts to quaint boutique retreats, affordable lodging, hostels, guesthouses, and vacation rentals. We will go into each category in this extensive guide, offering thorough details, suggestions, and average costs to assist you in making an informed choice for your stay in Brazil.

Upscale inns and resorts

Brazil offers an excellent range of five-star hotels and resorts that appeal to affluent tourists looking for extravagance, first-rate service, and top-notch amenities. The nation offers a number of opportunities to luxuriate in opulent comfort, whether you're searching for a beachside getaway or an urban hideaway. Here are a few notable examples of luxurious lodgings:

a) Rio de Janeiro's Copacabana Palace This legendary hotel, which is located on Copacabana Beach, is known for its ageless elegance, breathtaking vistas, and first-rate service. It has opulent accommodations, a spa, gourmet dining options, and a posh pool area.

b) Fasano So Paulo (So Paulo): This chic hotel is recognized for its cutting-edge style, sumptuous decor, and a rooftop pool with sweeping city views. It also has a chic bar and a highly regarded Italian restaurant.

c) Belmond Hotel das Cataratas (Foz do Iguaçu): This luxurious resort offers unmatched access to the beautiful Iguazu Falls and is situated inside Iguaçu National Park. An inviting ambiance is created by the hotel's attractive colonial-style building, rich grounds, and first-rate services.

Design-focused boutique hotels

Boutique and design hotels are the perfect option for tourists looking for distinctive and fashionable lodgings that capture Brazil's colorful culture and artistic flair. These establishments frequently offer attentive service, creative architecture, and a unique atmosphere. Here are a few standout choices:

Emiliano Rio, from Rio de Janeiro. Emiliano Rio combines elegance with a laid-back beachfront atmosphere with its modern architecture and opulent decor. The hotel features large rooms, an elegant restaurant, a spa, and an infinity pool on the rooftop.

b) Casa Turquesa (Paraty): This boutique hotel charms visitors with its lovely decor, bright accents, and kind welcome. It is located in the colonial town of Paraty. The hotel has individually designed rooms, a lovely courtyard, and a delicious breakfast.

c) UXUA Casa Hotel & Spa (Trancoso): Located in the artistic community of Trancoso,

UXUA features a diverse Brazilian style that combines rustic and modern elements. Private casas (houses), a spa, a restaurant, and verdant gardens are all part of the property.

Affordable Accommodations

In Brazil, travelers on a tight budget will discover a variety of inexpensive lodging options, including guesthouses, low-cost hotels, and hostels. While these choices might not have opulent features, they nonetheless offer cozy accommodations at reasonable costs. Here are some suggestions:

Pousada Casa Rosa in Florianópolis, to start: This warm inn in Florianópolis provides comfortable lodgings, a shared kitchen, and a garden area. It's a wonderful option for vacationers on a tight budget because of its accessible location close to the city center and well-liked beaches.

b) Hotel Galicia (Salvador): This inexpensive hotel offers straightforward, spotless rooms right in the middle of Salvador's historic district. It has a convenient location that makes it simple to reach popular attractions and a thriving local culture.

c) El Misti Hostel in Rio de Janeiro: This hostel is well-known for its welcoming environment and reasonable rates, and it provides both private rooms and dormitory-style lodging. Additionally, it arranges social events, making it a great choice for backpackers and lone travelers.

Guesthouses and Hostels

Young travelers, backpackers, and those seeking to interact with like-minded adventurers will find Brazil's hostels and guesthouses to be very welcoming and affordable. These lodgings frequently have common areas, communal kitchens, and planned activities. Here are a few standout choices:

Hostel Che Lagarto in Florianópolis, to start: This hostel, which is located near the beach, has a lively atmosphere and a variety of lodging choices, including dorms and private rooms. A bar, a pool, and frequent entertainment events are included.

b) Casa do Amarelindo (Salvador): Combining the benefits of a guesthouse with a boutique hotel, Casa do Amarelindo offers a quaint and cozy location in the middle of Salvador's historic district. It provides welcoming accommodations, a rooftop terrace, and attentive service.

The bohemian Santa Teresa district is home to the Books Hostel in Rio de Janeiro, which is distinguished by its literary-themed design and laid-back vibe. It has welcoming dorms, a common kitchen, a library, and a lovely garden.

Holiday Rentals

Apartments, homes, and villas available for rent on vacation offer a home-away-from-home experience, offering additional room, privacy, and the chance to fully enjoy the local way of life. Brazil's towns and coastal resorts provide a wide selection of vacation rental possibilities. Here are a few well-liked options:

Airbnb (a) Brazil has a wide range of vacation rental options available on the Airbnb platform, from quaint apartments in cities to beachside properties. While taking advantage of the ease of self-catering facilities, you can select accommodations that are customized to your needs and financial situation.

b) Vrbo: Vacation Rentals by Owner (Vrbo) offers a variety of getaway properties, including beach houses, mountain retreats, and apartments in the city. You can use a variety of parameters to narrow down your search for the ideal rental based on features, price, and neighborhood.

Rental agencies are available across Brazil and many of them specialize in vacation rentals, especially in well-known locations like Rio de Janeiro, Florianópolis, and Bios. These organizations provide individualized assistance in locating and reserving the best accommodation for your trip.

Average cost of lodging

The location, time of year, and kind of lodging all affect the average cost of lodging in Brazil. It's crucial to remember that the prices listed here are an estimate and could vary. The following are the typical nightly rates as of the time of writing:

- *$300-$800+ for luxury hotels and resorts*
- *$150 to $400 for boutique and design hotels*
- *Low-cost lodging: $50 to $100*
- *$20 to $60 for hostels and guesthouses*
- *Rentals for holidays: $70-$200*

You may find a wide variety of lodging alternatives in Brazil to fit any traveler's preferences and budget. Brazil has accommodations for every budget, including five-star hotels, upscale retreats, hostels, guesthouses, and vacation rentals. Indulgence, cultural immersion, affordability, or social connections—whatever your travel preferences—you can discover the ideal lodging while visiting Brazil's diverse and alluring landscapes.

Chapter 7: Itinerary for Two Weeks

The most populous nation in South America, Brazil, is a riveting travel destination that provides a dazzling fusion of natural marvels, cultural richness, and exhilarating adventures. Brazil has something to offer every traveler, from the alluring Amazon rainforest to the gorgeous beaches. We will take you on an exciting journey through Brazil in this thorough two-week itinerary, emphasizing its most famous locations and offering suggestions for each stop along the way.

Rio de Janeiro on Days 1-3

Rio de Janeiro, also known as the "Cidade Maravilhosa" (Magnificent City), is a bustling city tucked away between beautiful mountains and breathtaking beaches. Start your trip to Brazil by touring Rio's famous neighborhoods. Start by paying a visit to the renowned Christ the

Redeemer statue, which is perched atop Corcovado Mountain and provides sweeping views of the city. Next, proceed to Santa Teresa, a hipster neighborhood renowned for its quaint streets, galleries, and historic bars.

Without visiting Copacabana and Ipanema beaches and taking in their energetic ambiance, a trip to Rio de Janeiro would be incomplete. Enjoy a day of beach relaxation, mouthwatering caipirinhas, and getting to know the local beach culture. Take the cable car to Sugarloaf Mountain for a distinctive viewpoint of the city's spectacular sunset.

Tijuca National Park, the largest urban forest in the world, offers hiking trails that lead to amazing vistas and magnificent waterfalls for adventure seekers. Don't pass up the opportunity to enjoy Rio's vibrant nightlife, which features samba clubs and live music venues all across the city.

4-6 days: Salvador

Fly to Salvador, the vivacious capital of Bahia, which is renowned for its illustrious Afro-Brazilian culture and historic colonial buildings. A must-see destination is Pelourinho's historic center, a UNESCO World Heritage site. Wander the vibrant streets lined with baroque churches, pastel-colored structures, and bustling squares. Enjoy the delectable acarajé and moqueca meals while immersing yourself in the fascinating rhythms of capoeira.

Visit the nearby island of Itaparica for a day trip where you can unwind on lovely beaches and engage in water activities like sailing or snorkeling. Don't pass up the chance to listen to the throbbing sounds of samba, reggae, and axé music at one of the bustling music places Salvador has to offer.

Manaus and the Amazon Rainforest, days 7-9

Fly to Manaus to see the delights of this unrivaled natural ecosystem. Manaus is the entrance to the Amazon rainforest. Take a boat excursion down the Amazon River to see the stunning confluence of the sand-colored Solimes and the black Rio Negro rivers, which flow side by side for kilometres without interacting.

Experienced local guides will accompany you on guided hikes through the deep jungle as they reveal the rainforest's mysteries. Discover a variety of species, such as curious pink river dolphins, eye-catching macaws, and secretive jaguars. Spend a night at a remote eco-lodge where you can listen to the sounds of nature as you sleep and wake up to the chorus of howling monkeys.

Participate in indigenous villages to learn about their distinctive culture, customs, and close relationship to the rainforest. Enjoy canoeing through the constricting tributaries, swimming in the clean rivers, and basking in the spectacular sunsets over the huge Amazon.

Iguazu Falls, Day 10–12

Prepare to be amazed as you fly to Foz do Iguaçu and see the magnificent Iguazu Falls. This natural wonder is a UNESCO World Heritage site, and it is situated on the border of Brazil, Argentina, and Paraguay. Spend a day exploring the falls on the Brazilian side by strolling along well-kept pathways that provide breathtaking all-encompassing views of the cascades. As you get closer to the impressive Devil's Throat, the park's biggest waterfall, you can feel the mist on your face.

You may get up close to the falls and stroll along elevated walkways that will take you right into the heart of this natural wonder if you cross over to the Argentine side. Don't miss the thrilling boat trip beneath the falls, where you'll get a special view of Iguazu's force and beauty.

Consider taking a thrilling zipline trip through the nearby lush forests or taking a helicopter flight over the falls if you're looking for adventure. Enjoy Foz do Iguaçu's exciting nightlife and excellent local cuisine at night.

13-14th day: So Paulo

Visit the vibrant megacity and Brazilian cultural center of So Paulo to cap off your travels in Brazil. Explore the colorful street art, chic shops, and upmarket restaurants that can be found in Vila Madalena and Jardins, two thriving areas. Visit the MAPS in So Paulo, which houses a huge collection of masterpieces from Europe and Latin America.

Enjoy the numerous gastronomic experiences available in So Paulo's renowned gastronomy scene, which is influenced by cultures from all over the world. Don't miss the Mercado Municipal, a food market where you may enjoy regional specialties from Brazil like pastel and feijoada. Visit a bustling pub in the city and listen to live music, or visit the So Paulo Municipal Theater to see a show.

If you have the time, think about taking a day trip to the neighboring cities of Santos or Guarujá, where you can unwind on gorgeous beaches and engage in water activities like surfing or stand-up paddleboarding.

Brazil is a fascinating place with a wide variety of activities available, from discovering the energetic cities to getting lost in the wonders of the Amazon rainforest and the breathtaking Iguazu Falls. This two-week tour gives travelers a taste of the nation's diverse cultural legacy, stunning natural surroundings, and exciting outdoor activities. But Brazil has a lot more to offer, so feel free to stay longer or alter the itinerary to suit your preferences. Set out on this exciting adventure around Brazil to make unforgettable experiences in this alluring South American treasure.

Chapter 8: Markets and Shopping

Brazil is a dynamic nation renowned for its rich history, diverse culture, and distinctive artistic traditions. Brazil has a wide variety of shopping opportunities, from regional arts and crafts to memories and souvenirs. Popular retail areas may be explored, local handicrafts can be found, and open-air markets can be visited to experience the vibrant environment. We will go into these facets of purchasing in Brazil in this post, offering more details, suggestions, and advice on how to haggle politely.

Local crafts and artwork

Brazil is well known for its superb indigenous arts and crafts, which highlight the nation's originality and cultural heritage. There are many different artistic disciplines that have been handed down through the decades, from detailed woodwork to handcrafted pottery. "Barroco" pottery, which has its roots in the northeastern state of Bahia, is one of the most well-known artistic styles. The striking hues and distinctive patterns of ceramics make it a popular tourist item.

Wooden sculpture creation is another amazing Brazilian specialty. Visitors can find wonderful wooden sculptures created by gifted artists in the state of Minas Gerais, particularly in the city of Ouro Preto. These statues are meticulously carved, showing amazing attention to detail, and frequently feature religious figures.

Brazilian embroidery is an essential sight for everyone with an interest in textiles. In this age-old craft, elaborate motifs are made on fabric using colorful threads. Rio de Janeiro is well-known for its embroidery, and tourists can buy lovely stitched items that make for treasured keepsakes.

Gifts and Memorabilia

Brazil has a huge selection of memories and souvenirs that perfectly represent the spirit of the nation. Here are some suggestions:

These recognizable Brazilian flip-flops, known as "Havaianas," are not only cozy but also a representation of the country's beach culture. They are a stylish and useful souvenir because they are available in a range of hues and patterns.

Cachaça: As the national spirit of Brazil, cachaça is a well-liked option for travelers looking for a distinctive alcoholic drink to take home. It is manufactured from sugarcane and tastes well on its own or in cocktails.

Jewelry and gemstones: Brazil is renowned for producing valuable stones including amethyst, topaz, and tourmaline. These diamonds can be found in magnificent jewelry pieces that make for a timeless and refined souvenir.

Brazilian coffee is well-known for its premium beans and is one of the world's major manufacturers of the beverage. You may enjoy the tastes of Brazil long after your stay if you bring back a bag of Brazilian coffee.

Favored shopping areas

Brazil has a number of bustling shopping areas that welcome all types of customers. Here are a few well-known ones to check out:

Rua Oscar Freire in So Paulo is well-known for its upmarket boutiques and designer shops. It is situated in the affluent Jardins district. Along this tree-lined lane, fashion aficionados will discover a wealth of high-end brands and stylish stores.

Rua das Pedras in Buzios is a bustling street lined with boutiques, eateries, and art galleries. Bzios is a picturesque coastal village. It is a great location to find beachwear, regional crafts, and one-of-a-kind gifts.

Rio de Janeiro's Feira Hippie de Ipanema: The Feira Hippie de Ipanema is a weekly event that takes place on the city's coastline every Sunday. This outdoor market is a veritable gold mine of handcrafted goods, including jewelry, apparel, and artwork. It's the perfect place to experience the city's bohemian atmosphere.

Native American Crafts

There are several indigenous cultures in Brazil, and each has its own distinct artistic traditions. These groups create beautiful handicrafts that pay homage to their cultural history. Visitors may help keep the traditions and ways of life of the indigenous people by buying their goods. Here are some examples of native crafts to keep an eye out for:

Indigenous peoples with excellent weaving abilities include the Ashaninka and Yanomami. Using natural fibers and complex weaving techniques, they produce lovely baskets, purses, and hammocks.

Ceramics: The pottery skills of the Tapajós and Marajoara people are well-known. Their clay works frequently include intricate patterns and designs that draw inspiration from nature and native symbols.

Kayapó and Karajá tribes are well-known for their magnificent feather art. Their elaborate headdresses, masks, and ceremonial ornaments, which display their strong spiritual ties to nature, are made from colorful bird feathers.

Outdoor markets

The Brazilian tradition of "," or open-air markets, is deeply ingrained. These bustling markets provide a distinctive shopping experience where customers can engage with sellers face-to-face, learn about regional customs, and find hidden treasures. The following Brazilian open-air markets are noteworthy:

One of the biggest open-air marketplaces in Latin America is found in the city of Belém, which is located in the northern state of Pará. With a wide variety of fruits, vegetables, spices, and local goods, it is a sensory delight. Additionally, local specialties, handicrafts, and herbal treatments are available to tourists.

Rio de Janeiro 's Feira de São Cristóvão: This thriving market in Rio de Janeiro honors the northeastern Brazilian regions culture. It offers a wide variety of food stalls, live musical performances, and merchants offering artisanal goods like jewelry, apparel, and crafts.

Feira de Artesanato da Praia de Pajuçara, Maceió: This beachside market is a great place to find regional handicrafts like woven goods, pottery, and artwork. It is located in the city of Maceió, in the state of Alagoas. The market offers a charming environment with mesmerizing sea views.

Etiquette and Tips for Bargaining

Brazilian marketplaces sometimes involve bartering, so being aware of a few etiquette rules and recommendations will improve your buying experience. Here are a few suggestions:

Engage in Amical Negotiation: In Brazil, bargaining is typically done in an amical style. Start by expressing sincere interest in the merchandise and strike up a pleasant dialog with the vendor. This builds a relationship that might result in better offers.

Compare Prices: It's a good idea to look around and compare prices at other stalls or shops before deciding on a price for something. As a result, you have a clearer idea of the market worth and are more equipped to negotiate.

Be Respectful: It's important to maintain respect during haggling and refrain from criticizing the item or the vendor. Keep in mind that haggling is a cultural custom, and that being upbeat helps create a nice purchasing experience.

Set Boundaries: Before entering into discussions, decide on your spending limit and the highest price you are willing to pay for a product. Striking a balance between receiving a reasonable price and assisting regional craftspeople is crucial.

Learn Some Basic Portuguese Phrases: Getting along with the merchant might be facilitated by learning a few simple Portuguese phrases. Simple greetings and gestures of gratitude can improve both sides' enjoyment of the negotiation process.

Shopping in Brazil provides a wealth of chances to discover regional arts and crafts, acquire one-of-a-kind trinkets, and immerse oneself in the energetic atmosphere of open-air markets. Brazil offers a variety of shopping options, from high-end stores to handcrafted goods made by indigenous people. Visitors may easily traverse the shopping experience and make treasured purchases by adhering to local norms and using bargaining techniques. So be ready to indulge in the varied shopping delights that Brazil has to offer whether you're wandering through the streets of So Paulo or exploring the markets of Belém.

Chapter 9: Health and safety Information

Brazil is a vibrant, multicultural nation renowned for its breathtaking scenery, illustrious history, and cordial friendliness. To ensure a smooth and enjoyable journey, it is necessary to be aware of health and safety precautions, just like when visiting any other place. We will cover a variety of topics in this thorough guide, including health precautions and vaccinations, emergency services and hospitals, travel insurance, the safety of water and food, crime awareness and prevention, as well as natural hazards and safety measures.

Medical Precautions and Vaccinations

It is crucial to speak with a healthcare provider or travel medicine expert before leaving for Brazil to go over the essential vaccines and safety measures. Depending on the length of your trip, your intended destinations within Brazil, and your particular medical history, different vaccinations may be advised. However, it is typically advised that visitors to Brazil get the following shots:

Ensure you are currently on routine vaccinations such as measles, mumps, and rubella (MMR), diphtheria, tetanus, and pertussis, varicella (chickenpox), polio, and the annual flu shot.

Hepatitis A: Due to Brazil's moderate risk of contracting hepatitis A, this vaccination is advised for all visitors to the country. Usually, it spreads by tainted food or drink.

Typhoid: This vaccination is advised, especially if you intend to consume street food or travel to unsanitary places.

Brazil is seen as a nation where there is a chance that yellow fever will spread in some areas. Visitors to these locations, including the Pantanal wetlands and Amazon rainforest, are advised to get the immunization. If you have recently visited Brazil, several nations may also demand proof of yellow fever vaccine upon admission.

Other immunizations: Depending on your travel plans, you should also think about getting immunized against diseases including hepatitis B, rabies, and meningitis.

It is best to plan your vaccination appointments well in advance of your travel, as some vaccinations may need to be administered more than once or may take some time to take effect. Furthermore, think about packing a compact vacation medical kit that includes essentials like painkillers, anti-diarrhea medication, and insect repellent.

Hospital emergency services

Knowing how to get emergency services and where to find nearby hospitals is essential in the event of a medical emergency in Brazil. In Brazil, dialing 192 will link you to the Unified

Health System (SUS), which is the number for emergencies. However, keep in mind that there can be a shortage of English-speaking operators, so it can be useful to have a Portuguese-speaking friend or utilize translation software.

Major cities also have private hospitals and clinics that provide speedier and higher-quality medical services. They frequently have English-speaking employees and are more accustomed to working with patients from other countries. To guarantee that you receive the necessary care without incurring significant costs, it is imperative that you have travel insurance that covers medical emergencies and hospitalization.

Travel Protection

When visiting Brazil, it is strongly advised to purchase travel insurance as it offers financial security and peace of mind in the event of unforeseen circumstances like medical emergencies, trip cancellations, or lost luggage.

The following elements should be taken into account when choosing a travel insurance plan:

Medical Insurance: Check to see if the insurance covers medical costs, emergency medical transportation, and repatriation of remains.

Look for coverage that pays out non-refundable charges in the event that your vacation is canceled or interrupted due to unforeseeable events like illness, injury, or natural disasters.

Choosing a policy that covers lost or stolen luggage, personal items, or travel papers will help you avoid having your belongings taken advantage of.

Check if the insurance provider provides round-the-clock assistance services, such as a helpline you may call in case of emergencies or if you need information about a trip.

Food and Water Safety

To avoid digestive disorders in Brazil, it is crucial to exercise caution when it comes to the safety of the food and water supply. For a risk-free dining experience, heed these advice:

Water: It's not always a good idea to drink tap water in Brazil. It is recommended to drink bottled water or to boil the tap water first. Additionally, when brushing your teeth, use bottled water.

Food: Steer clear of seafood, eggs, and raw or undercooked meats. Pick produce that can be fully washed with safe water or that can be peeled. Although enticing, make sure that the street food is prepared and cooked in hygienic conditions.

Drinks: Be cautious while consuming ice in beverages because it could have been created with tap water. Stay with bottled, canned, or boiled water-prepared beverages.

Restaurants: When dining out, pick reputed places that adhere to good sanitary standards. Look for areas that are crowded and have received favorable evaluations from both residents and visitors.

Crime Prevention and Awareness

Despite the fact that Brazil is a stunning country, it is crucial to be aware of potential hazards related to crime and take the appropriate precautions to protect personal safety. Here are some pointers to keep you secure:

Be Alert in Public: Keep a watchful eye on your possessions, particularly in crowded places like markets, transit hubs, and tourist destinations. Avoid flashing expensive items or big amounts of cash by carrying your valuables in a money belt or a covert bag.

Transit Security: Be aware of your surroundings when utilizing public transit, and stay away from going alone late at night, especially in new regions. Avoid using unmarked vehicles and instead use licensed taxis or ride-hailing services.

Keep up-to-date: Learn about the neighborhoods' reputations for safety before visiting, and stay away from those with a history of high crime. Keep abreast of the most recent travel warnings and heed the guidance of local authorities.

Blend In: Steer clear of displaying dazzling jewelry or expensive attire that can draw unwanted attention. To reduce the chance of standing out as a prospective target, dress modestly and conform to the local way of life.

Hotel Safety: Pick places to stay that are respected and safe. Make sure the locks on your hotel room are strong, and think about employing extra security tools like door wedges or portable door alarms.

Safety precautions and natural hazards

Brazil is a country with a variety of beautiful natural landscapes, but it is also vulnerable to many natural disasters. Learn about the possible risks and implement the necessary safety measures:

Landslides and floods: Some parts of Brazil, especially during the rainy season, may experience landslides and floods. Keep up with weather reports and heed local authorities' recommendations. Avoid locations that are prone to flooding and exercise caution when using roads or trails during periods of intense rain.

Mosquito-Borne Diseases: Dengue fever, the Zika virus, and chikungunya are among the mosquito-borne illnesses that are prevalent in Brazil. Wear long sleeves and pants, use insect repellents containing DEET, and sleep under mosquito nets, especially in places with a lot of mosquitoes.

Beach safety: Brazil has beautiful beaches, but it's necessary to swim carefully. Be aware of strong currents or riptides, pay heed to warning signs, and swim only in places where lifeguards are present. If unsure of the state of the water, seek guidance from local officials or seasoned surfers.

Wildlife Encounters: A variety of animals, including poisonous snakes and spiders, can be found in Brazil. Wear adequate footwear, stay on designated trails, and avoid touching or upsetting animals when exploring natural areas. Seek emergency medical assistance if you have been bitten or stung.

Sun protection is important because of the country's tropical environment. Wear sunscreen with a high SPF, cover up with hats and sunglasses, and look for shade during the warmest parts of the day to protect your skin.

Although traveling to Brazil might be enthralling, it's crucial to put your health and safety first. Make sure you have the required immunizations, that you have travel insurance, and that you are aware of any potential risks. You may have fun while visiting Brazil while reducing potential health and safety risks by adhering to these recommendations and using caution.

Chapter 10: Festivals and Cultural Experiences

Brazil is a multicultural nation with a wide range of experiences available that highlight its colorful heritage. Brazil has much to offer for the culture vulture, from Carnival celebrations to trips to indigenous communities, Samba schools, and religious festivals. In this article, we'll go in-depth on each of these cultural encounters and offer more details and suggestions for an amazing immersion in Brazilian culture.

Carnival festivities

Unquestionably, one of Brazil's most well-known and eagerly awaited celebrations, Carnival draws millions of tourists from all over the world. It is a colorful and opulent occasion that occurs in the days before Lent, usually in early February or March. Rio de Janeiro, So Paulo, Salvador, and Recife host the country's largest Carnival celebrations, while numerous other cities also hold their own distinctive versions of the carnival.

Carnival in Rio de Janeiro is especially well-known for its splendor and spectacle. The samba schools in the city spend months meticulously preparing their extravagant floats, stunning costumes, and vivacious dance performances for the Sambadrome. The Sambadrome is a specially constructed parade avenue where the top-performing samba schools vie for honors. Anyone visiting Rio during Carnival must attend a Sambadrome parade. You will become completely engrossed in the festival's joyful attitude thanks to the vigor, colors, and contagious rhythms.

The Carnival in Sao Paulo is another spectacular event. It may not be as well known as Rio's Carnival, but it nevertheless has a huge procession with many different samba schools. The city's samba schools put on enthralling shows and gorgeous floats to display their skills and ingenuity. Serious samba fans who value the technical qualities of the performances are known to flock to So Paulo's Carnival.

Salvador's Carnival celebrations differ from those elsewhere. The sounds of Afro-Brazilian music and dance fill the streets here. There is a buzz in the air as the trios elétricos (huge trucks with powerful sound systems) bring well-known musicians and bands through the streets. Both locals and visitors take part in the celebrations, dancing to the beat of the axé music and joining in the renowned trio (street parades). Compared to the parades in Rio and Sao Paulo, this experience is more interactive and participatory.

Brazil's northern cities of Recife and Olinda, noted for their cultural and historical significance, offer a distinctive Carnival experience. In Olinda, locals and tourists gather to celebrate in a more private and traditional setting as the streets are filled with traditional maracatu and frevo music. Contrarily, Recife holds enormous outdoor gatherings called where people dance to the lively beats of frevo and other regional rhythms.

If you have the chance to enjoy Carnival in Brazil, we advise you to make travel arrangements well in advance. Early reservations are advised for lodging and or Sambadrome tickets because they frequently sell out. Be ready for enormous crowds and be sure to join the locals in their joyful celebrations to fully immerse yourself in the festivities.

Capoeira Performances

Afro-Brazilian capoeira is a distinctive martial art that incorporates dance, acrobatics, and music. It was created by Africans who were held as slaves during the colonial era as a dance-like method of self-defense. Capoeira has developed into a modern cultural manifestation that represents tenacity, flexibility, and originality.

Watching a capoeira demonstration is an amazing experience that lets you see the physical prowess and artistic ability of the capoeiristas, the practitioners. The dancers and musicians form a circle for the , when the moves are done as a joyful dialogue of kicks, sweeps, and flips. The tempo of the game is set by the rhythm of the berimbau, a melodic bow, while additional instruments and chanting support the action.

Capoeira performances are regularly held in public spaces, parks, and cultural institutions throughout Brazil, but especially in Salvador and Rio de Janeiro. For tourists who are interested in learning the fundamentals of this engaging art form, many capoeira schools also offer classes or workshops. Attending a class can be educational since it gives you a better understanding of the physicality, philosophy, and history of capoeira.

Recommendation: To discover capoeira courses and demonstrations, check with regional cultural institutions, get referrals from locals, or look out capoeira schools online in the region you're visiting. If you decide to take part in a demonstration or lesson, do so with courtesy and in accordance with the roda's rules of conduct. Keep in mind that capoeira is more than just a martial art; for the Afro-Brazilian population, it has great cultural and historical value.

Visits to Indigenous Communities

Numerous indigenous communities exist in Brazil, each with its own distinct culture, traditions, and way of life. Visits to these communities offer a chance to learn about their complex histories, ecological practices, spiritual beliefs, and social systems.

Given that it contains the greatest number of different indigenous groups in Brazil, the Amazon rainforest region is extremely crucial for indigenous communities. The Amazon is home to numerous tribes, including the Yanomami, Kayapó, Ashaninka, and Tikuna. Numerous of these villages are open to tourists who want to learn about their way of life and contribute to the preservation of their cultural heritage.

You might have the opportunity to partake in customary ceremonies, discover medicinal plants and their curative virtues, see handicraft demonstrations, and engage in cultural interactions with locals when visiting an indigenous community. These encounters provide a rare chance to understand the complex interaction of indigenous peoples with the environment, as well as their profound understanding of the natural world and sustainable lifestyles.

It is crucial to approach trips to indigenous communities with respect, humility, and an open mind. It is vital to conduct ethical and ecological tourism while assisting neighborhood-based projects that put indigenous peoples' welfare and self-determination first.

It is advised to use trustworthy tour operators or groups that have forged alliances with the communities to plan a visit to an indigenous community. These groups make sure that visits are carried out respectfully and responsibly, putting the community's residents' welfare first. Keep in mind cultural sensitivities while visiting and always abide by the rules and regulations established by the community.

Samba Music and Schools

The music and dancing style known as samba is frequently referred to as the "soul of Brazil" and is firmly woven into the national identity. It was created in the Afro-Brazilian communities and has since come to represent the pride and uniqueness of the country. Samba dance is distinguished by its vivacious motions, hip swaying, and intricate footwork, while samba music is distinguished by its contagious rhythms, lively percussion, and beautiful harmonies.

Samba schools, which unite musicians, dancers, and aficionados to celebrate and uphold the samba culture, are social and cultural organizations. They are very important during Carnival because they participate in ornate parades at the Sambadrome. Samba schools, on the other hand, are active all year round, planning practices, shows, and cultural events.

A wonderful approach to become fully immersed in the dynamic world of samba is to attend a samba school rehearsal. The public is invited to watch the , or rehearsals, which provide a real look at the samba's music, movement, and sense of community. You can get down on the floor and dance along with the others, pick up a few samba moves, or just take in the exciting atmosphere and live performances.

Recommendation: Check local cultural centers, look at event listings, or ask locals for recommendations to locate samba schools and attend rehearsals. Don't be afraid to join in the dancing and be ready to embrace the samba's rhythmic and energizing nature. Keep in mind that the samba is a celebration of joy and camaraderie, so have fun and be silly!

Folk dances and traditional music

Folklore and traditional dances in Brazil provide a window onto the nation's rich cultural past and regional identities. Every region has its own distinctive dances and musical genres that are a reflection of its history, native influences, and immigration trends.

The Forró is a well-known traditional dance that has its roots in northeastern Brazil. Partner dance called forró is performed to the sounds of accordion, zabumba (bass drum), and triangle. Fast footwork and close physical touch between the dancers define it. Forró is popular in forró pé-de-serra, which are traditional dance halls where locals and tourists congregate to dance the night away.

The Chula is a unique dance style performed by gauchos (cowboys) in the southern part of Brazil. Gauchos in traditional garb including ponchos, wide-brimmed hats, and leather boots perform the mesmerizing chula dance. The dance, which incorporates rhythmic footwork, hand gestures, and spinning movements, is an exhibition of agility and coordination.

The Maculelê Afro-Brazilian dance form is prominent in the state of Bahia. Maculelê is a performance art that uses wooden sticks or machetes and has its roots in African slave traditions. Dancers do a choreographed routine in which they move in tandem and beat the sticks simultaneously. A fascinating visual and audio experience is produced by the chanting and energetic, rhythmic motions.

These are just a few of the numerous traditional dances that can be seen all around Brazil. The Carimbó in the Amazon, the Frevo in Pernambuco, and the Catira in the Midwest are just a few examples of the distinctive dances that are specific to each region.

Consult local event calendars, cultural centers, or dance studios to learn about traditional dances in your region of Brazil. Folk dance festivals and performances that bring together numerous traditional dance ensembles are held in several cities. Don't be reluctant to join and pick up a few fundamental skills because it will enhance your immersion experience and connection to the community.

Religious Celebrations and Festivals

Brazilian religions are diverse and influenced by indigenous, African, and European cultures. Religious celebrations and ceremonies offer insight into the spiritual practices and beliefs of various communities as well as a peep into the syncretism that distinguishes religious life in Brazil.

The Festa de Iemanjá, which is observed on February 2nd in several coastal cities, is one well-known religious holiday. This event honors the sea goddess Iemanjá, an Afro-Brazilian divinity. In addition to flowers, candles, and little boats laden with donations to be released into the water as a symbol of thanks and petitions for blessings, devotees assemble at beaches while wearing all-white clothing.

The Cristo de Nazaré, which takes place in October in Belém, Para, is another important religious occasion. Millions of pilgrims from all across Brazil participate in this Catholic procession honoring Nossa Senhora de Nazaré (Our Lady of Nazareth). The Trasladaço, a large procession in which a statue of the Virgin Mary is carried through the streets while being attended by tens of thousands of worshippers, is the event's high point.

The Lavagem do Bonfim is a religious and cultural celebration held in Salvador in January. The steps leading to the Bonfim Church are ritualistically washed as part of this ceremony. Participants clean the steps while singing and dancing to the beat of the drums while wearing white clothing and carrying pitchers of fragrant water.

These religious celebrations and rituals provide a rare window into the synthesis of African, native, and European traditions that form Brazilian society. They offer a chance to observe the fervor, spirituality, and ties of community that are essential to the religious lives of many Brazilians.

Recommendation: If you have the opportunity to attend a religious festival or ceremony in Brazil, get to know the traditions and protocol surrounding the occasion. Be cognizant of the significance these events hold for the participants and respect the rites' solemnity. It's important to embrace these occasions with respect and openness since they are manifestations of faith and dedication.

Brazil's festivals and cultural experiences offer a rich tapestry of customs, music, dance, and spirituality. Brazil encourages you to fully immerse yourself in its rich cultural legacy, which includes the majesty of Carnival, the rhythmic pulses of samba, the creativity of capoeira, the richness of indigenous cultures, the enchantment of traditional dances, and the spiritual depth of religious festivals. Plan your trip, respect the customs of the area, and give in to the contagious spirit and kindness that characterize Brazil's cultural landscape.

Chapter 11: Brazil Practical Details

The largest nation in South America, Brazil, is renowned for its vivacious culture, magnificent scenery, and kind hospitality. It's important to equip yourself with some useful facts before visiting Brazil in order to make the most of your trip and ensure a positive experience.

Visa Requirements: You could require a visa to enter Brazil depending on your nationality. It's crucial to research the necessary visas well in advance and apply for the right visa category. For comprehensive information, you can check the website of the Brazilian Embassy or Consulate in your nation.

Currency and Exchange: The Brazilian Real (BRL) is the country's legal tender. Before your travel or when you arrive at the airport, it is important to exchange some money. Additionally, ATMs, which are extensively dispersed in cities and tourist hotspots, allow you to withdraw cash. Although most businesses take credit cards, it's still a good idea to have some cash on hand for smaller purchases or in case of emergencies.

Brazil is typically a safe place to travel to, but as with any trip, it's vital to exercise some caution. Be careful where you go, especially in crowded areas, avoid flashing precious jewelry or electronics, and only use dependable transportation. For any additional advice on specific safety precautions related to your destination in Brazil, it is also advised to speak with local authorities or reliable sources.

Portuguese is the official language of Brazil. Although English may be used in popular tourist destinations and hotels, it's helpful to acquire a few fundamental Portuguese idioms to get by in everyday situations. It will improve your experience when speaking with folks in more distant regions and the locals will appreciate your efforts.

Local traditions and manners

Brazilian culture is broad and rich, with its own set of traditions and manners. It will be easier for you to fit in and establish a deeper connection with the locals if you comprehend and respect these cultural standards. Here are some crucial manners and traditions guidelines to remember:

Regarding greetings and personal space, Brazilians are often welcoming and friendly. The most typical greeting is a handshake, however close friends and family members may also hug or kiss each other on the cheek. When interacting with natives, it's critical to respect personal space and refrain from intruding on it.

Brazilians approach time with a more loose attitude, and timeliness is not always rigidly enforced. It's typical for social events or unofficial meetings to begin a little beyond the scheduled time. For official events or business appointments, it is still advised to arrive on time.

Dining Etiquette: It is normal to bring a little gift, like flowers or a bottle of wine, after being asked to go to someone's home for dinner. Brazilians enjoy their food, and eating is frequently a communal and relaxing activity. It's polite to sample a little bit of everything offered and to thank the host for the delectable fare.

Beach Culture: Brazil is known for its beautiful beaches, and both natives and tourists enjoy relaxing by the water. Respecting regional traditions is crucial when visiting the beach. Brazilians are typically at ease with their bodies, although, unless in specially designated areas, it's more common to wear swimming suits than to go topless or nudist.

Portuguese phrases you should know

Your time in Brazil will be considerably enhanced and your interactions with locals will be more fun if you learn a few basic Portuguese phrases. Here are a few key words to get you going:

- *Greetings and Foundational Words:*
- *Olá! (Hello!)*
- *Good day! (Hello, good day!)*
- *Good morning! (Good day, everybody!)*
- *Good night! (Good night!)*
- *Thank you/Por favor/Obrigado Thank you.*
- *Requesting Directions:*
- *Where is...? (Where are you?)*
- *How do I get there? How can I get there?*
- *esquerda (to the left) (to the right)*
- *Reto (Go directly ahead)*
- *Getting Snacks and Drinks:*
- *I would want to, Eu gostaria de*
- *Please order from the menu, O cardápio.*
- *Water is gua.*
- *Coffee shop*
- *Please have a drink, uma cerveja*
- *How much does it cost? (What is the price?)*
- *Simple Emergency Words:*

- *Ajuda! (Help!)*
- *I require a medical professional.*
- *Where is the closest hospital located? (What hospital is the closest?)*

Climate and Travel Advice

The weather in Brazil varies considerably by region, so it's crucial to pack in accordance with the places you intend to go. Consider the following basic climate and packing advice:

The five primary climatic areas of Brazil are equatorial, tropical, semiarid, highland tropical, and subtropical. It is essential to examine the weather in your location during the time of your visit because every region has its own unique weather patterns.

Pack breathable, lightweight clothing for hot, humid climates like those found along the coast or in the Amazon rainforest. Bring warmer clothes for cooler areas, such as Brazil's southern highlands or the highlands itself. Don't forget to carry a hat, sunglasses, sunscreen, and comfortable walking shoes.

Rain Gear: The Amazon region of Brazil has significant annual precipitation. Packing a lightweight raincoat or umbrella is a good idea if you want to stay dry during unexpected downpours.

Insect repellent: Mosquitoes in tropical regions can be bothersome and may spread diseases like dengue fever or the Zika virus. Carry a bug repellent that contains DEET or another potent repellent, and use it frequently.

Outlets and Adapters for Electricity

The standard voltage and frequency in Brazil are 127V and 60Hz, respectively. The power outlets have three round pins and are type N. You will want a power adapter or voltage converter if your electrical equipment operates on a different voltage or has a different type of plug. Here are some pointers for Brazilian electrical outlets and adapters:

Power Adapters: You'll need a power adapter that works with Brazilian power outlets in order to use your electronic devices while traveling from abroad. Look for an adapter with a universal design that can fit multiple plug types or that can accommodate type N plugs.

Voltage Converters: If your gadgets run on a different voltage, like 220V, a voltage converter is also required to make sure they function properly and prevent harm. Before plugging anything in, check the voltage rating.

Availability of Adapters: Most electronics stores, travel supply shops, and online retailers sell power adapters and voltage converters. To make sure you have the necessary adapters when you need them, it is a good idea to buy them before your trip.

Communication and the Internet

Having access to the internet and being connected can significantly improve your trip experience in Brazil. Here are some details regarding online and telephone options:

Wi-Fi Accessibility: at large cities and popular tourist destinations, Wi-Fi is generally accessible at hotels, eateries, cafés, and shopping centers. Additionally, a lot of motels offer free WiFi to their visitors. However, Wi-Fi might not be as accessible in more rural or outlying areas.

SIM Cards & Mobile Data: You can buy a prepaid SIM card from one of Brazil's top mobile network providers, like Vivo, Claro, or TIM, to have constant internet access and make local calls. Airports, convenience stores, and the official retail locations of the network providers all carry these SIM cards. Ascertain that your mobile device is unlocked and appropriate for the regional network frequencies.

Internet cafes: If you don't own a mobile device or would rather use a computer, you can find one in most cities and popular tourist destinations.

For internet connectivity, these places often charge an hourly fee.

Travel apps and resources

There are numerous travel tools and smartphone apps that may help you with different elements of your vacation, making your trip to Brazil more easy and pleasurable. Here are a few suggestions:

Google Maps: For exploring Brazil's cities, towns, and attractions, Google Maps is a dependable and user-friendly software. It offers thorough maps, instructions, up-to-the-minute traffic data, and choices for public transit.

Duolingo is a well-known language-learning program that you may use to learn or hone your Portuguese language abilities. It provides interactive exercises and bite-sized lessons to help you learn the language's fundamentals.

iOverlander is a helpful tool for tourists who are exploring off-the-beaten-path locations in Brazil or taking part in activities like camping or road excursions. It offers details on campgrounds, gas stations, hostels, and other necessities.

TripAdvisor: TripAdvisor is a popular resource for finding lodging, dining, attractions, and trips. It provides user opinions, rankings, and suggestions to assist you in planning your vacation.

Mobile Banking applications: Think about installing the mobile banking applications offered by your bank if you have a local bank account or need to monitor your funds while in Brazil. You may use these applications to check your account balance, send payments, and handle other banking tasks while you're on the road.

You'll be well-equipped to explore the fascinating and diverse nation of Brazil if you become knowledgeable about relevant information, regional cultures, key words, the weather, and packing advice. Enjoy your journey and take in the fascinating culture and breathtaking scenery that lie ahead!

Conclusion

In conclusion, Brazil is a destination that provides the traveler with a full and dynamic vacation experience. Brazil has something for everyone, from its spectacular natural beauty to its vibrant cultural heritage. You will make lifelong memories if you embrace the colorful spirit of the nation.

Final advice and suggestions

Brazil is a stunning nation to see, but there are some safety precautions you should take. Be mindful of your surroundings, especially in crowded places, and keep expensive items hidden. To safeguard yourself and your possessions, use reputable transportation services and think about purchasing travel insurance.

Language: Because Portuguese is Brazil's national language, knowing a few fundamental words will help you interact with the population there. Brazilians value the effort, and it can significantly improve your trip.

Brazil has a variety of climates, so it's necessary to pack appropriately. Pack breathable, light clothing for the warmer locations and warmer layers for the cooler ones based on the weather forecast for your individual travel plans. For outdoor activities, don't forget to bring sunscreen, a hat, and insect repellent.

Currency and Exchange: The Brazilian Real (BRL) is the country's legal tender. It's a good idea to exchange some money before your trip or to use an ATM when you get there to get cash. Although credit cards are routinely accepted in big cities, it's always a good idea to have some cash on hand for smaller businesses or in farther-flung locations.

Accept Brazil's Dynamic Spirit

Immersing oneself in Brazil's colorful culture and energetic energy will significantly improve your travel experience. Here are some ideas for embracing Brazil's vivacious spirit:

Carnival: If you have the chance, don't miss Rio de Janeiro's renowned Carnival. This festival takes place every year and is a spectacle of vibrant parades, samba dancing, and energetic street celebrations. You will be amazed by this celebration of life, music, and dancing.

Brazil is the birthplace of the rhythmic musical genres bossa nova, samba, and others. Visit bustling clubs and pubs to dance the night away and learn more about the local music scene. To truly experience Brazil's contagious rhythms, take a samba lesson or sign up for a drumming session.

Local cuisine: Brazilian food is tasty and varied. Enjoy traditional fare including po de queijo (cheese bread), acarajé (deep-fried bean fritters), and feijoada (black bean stew). Try the caipirinha, the country's signature drink, which is created with cachaça (sugarcane liquor), lime, sugar, and ice.

Festivals & Celebrations: Brazil is a nation that loves to party, and you can discover a variety of festivals and events there all year long that highlight the nation's rich cultural heritage. There are constant celebrations in Brazil, from the Festa Junina in June to the Bumba Meu Boi in the Northeast.

Taking Stock of Your Journey

Take some time to consider your experiences and the memories you've made as your stay in Brazil comes to an end. Think about the following:

Natural Wonders: The Amazon Rainforest, Iguazu Falls, and the Pantanal wetlands are just a few of Brazil's breath-taking natural wonders. Consider how important it is to protect these areas for future generations given their breathtaking beauty.

Cultural Diversity: Brazil has an incredibly diverse population. Consider the richness and complexity of Brazilian culture and the lessons it has taught you about tolerance and acceptance, from the indigenous villages in the Amazon to the Afro-Brazilian roots in Bahia.

Personal Development: Going on a foreign trip frequently results in personal development and self-discovery. Consider the difficulties you overcame, the fresh viewpoints you attained, and how these events have molded you into the person you are now.

Tell Us About Your Travels

After experiencing Brazil's vivacious attitude, think about telling others about your travels. Your observations and recollections may encourage others to set out on their own Brazilian journey, whether it be through writing a blog, making a photo album, or simply sharing stories with friends and family.

Recognition & Credits

I would like to thank everyone who helped create this trip guide and the resources they provided. We would especially want to thank all of the visitors, residents, and specialists who contributed their insights and experiences regarding Brazil. Credit should also be given to the numerous travel blogs, publications, and articles that provide insightful advice and inspiration.

Boa Viagem e goodbye!

We bid you adieu and wish you a "boa " as your trip through Brazil draws to a close. May you carry with you the colorful energy of Brazil long after you return home. May your future travels be full of surprise, joy, and amazing experiences, whether you decide to return or see other parts of the world. Happy travels!

Printed in Great Britain
by Amazon